Husband & Wife Love Forgiveness I Do Romance Vows

Poetry Ring Of Marriage

Phyllis E. Griffin

Dear Heavenly Father,

I give you glory for your inspiration to write your book. I pray that you will use these words to bless marriages and to bless & encourage those who desire to be married in Jesus (Yeshua)'s name.

Amen.

Table of Content

Marriage-Marriage

Marriage... Marriage, what's it all about?
A man and woman not living in doubt
Believing that God has put them together
that one day, they'll both go to heaven

A little pout here and a little spat there
through it all, God's love, we share
One day you know we both said, "I do"
My brother, my sister we've been through

Both through the rain and through the pain
Through life's challenges, But God kept us sane
You see, my friend, marriage can be a beautiful thing
If we learn to trust in God and to Him we lean

Trust him... trust him in your decisions
That the devil won't put you in derision
Acknowledge him... acknowledge him in all your ways
for he will give you some delightful days

"Extra-Extra"

Extra, Extra, read all about it!
Marriage is not a myth, it is indeed legit

Starting in Genesis, going through Revelation,
you will find that marriage, is a part of God's
foundation

You see, marriage is both old and current news,
if you seek and learn, you might even be enthused

It's a relationship between, a man and a woman,
the Most High, Himself has ordained and summoned

He planned for it to last and last,
not to be yoked or bound to the past

If we learn how to follow the golden rule,
using God's wisdom and love as our tool

If we live each day to serve one another,
put God first, then each other

Then marriage can be a picture of heaven,
A part of God's creation of days of seven

A reflection of his love for mankind,
A reflection of his relationship by design

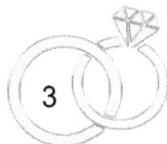

The world might say that it's old fogy,
However, when we look to God, it's a beautiful story

A story of two hearts turned into one,
A miracle made possible, by God's gracious son.

Extra, Extra, read all about it!
From every page you can learn a bit

From Genesis to Malachi, all the way through,
You'll find that God's concept of marriage really isn't
new

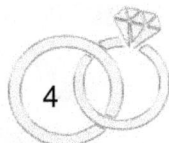

"I Said, I Do"

One day I said, 'I do'
So did you
We kissed and we hugged
We exchanged a ring
Not really knowing what the years would bring

We walked down the aisle to pledge our love
Believing that God who lived above
Would bless us and keep us
Under his cleansing blood

Now the years have come, the years have gone
We've had times of laughter and sometimes we've
mourned
However, through it all, we have known
That the God up above
        that sits on the throne
Has kept us and loved us
        with his amazing grace
Strengthened us,
        upheld us, so we could run this race
So, we said, "I do"
God has saw us through
Through every test and all the mess
And still today we say, yes!

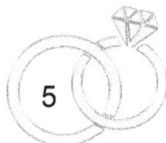

The Marriage Ring

The marriage ring is a sacred thing,
representing love and fidelity

In order to make its symbol work,
You must seek God's reality

The ring represents endless and unconditional love,
love is only possible from the Father who lives above

The marriage ring means, a solitary commitment to
just one,
A commitment that helps you firmly stand and not run,
run, run.

Some people spend hundreds and yes, even
thousands,
To put a ring on the finger of some man's daughter

Sometimes too much is spent on the ring itself,
While seeking marital wisdom is put on the shelf

Its value is not, in how much it cost
Instead ensuring, that the pure love isn't lost

It's not about how big the rock is, so we can have
bragging rights,
It's about making a decision, to be faithful, in the
Almighty God's sight

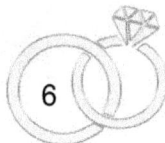

It's not about how much it sparkles against the sun,
Instead, how much you're willing to invest to have a good marital bond

The marriage ring serves as a reminder that, we're no longer single,
It helps to give Godly conviction, whenever we have to mingle

It says, I'm off limits because I've been spoken for,
It quickly says to a flirtation, I am not an open door

The marriage ring cannot stand alone, whenever we are approached,
We must be willing to speak up, whenever our pureness is encroached

Yes, the marriage ring is a sacred thing
That represents love and fidelity
However, its beauty goes beyond all myths and wedding formalities

The Marriage Bed

The marriage bed is a secret sacred place,
Where love is poured out by God's amazing grace

It is a place where two become one, only by his
design,
It is a place where spouses communicate, that you
are truly mine

The marriage bed is where you will experience love
completely
Unashamedly and deeply with your chosen sweetie

The marriage bed is a divine and precious mystery,
Where the two of you can create your very own
history

It is a place of consummation and devotion,
A place where love moves from notion to motion

The bible says that the marriage bed is undefiled,
But please my brother, my sister you need not be
beguiled

Honor and respect must stay in place,
As we indulge in this God-given grace

As we set forth to meet each other's needs,
Sharing our love, receiving and planting life seeds

We must honor the one that made our marriage
possible,
In every act, we must demonstrate that we are
responsible

Doing nothing that will dishonor him or our bodies of
glory,
Knowing that he is ever present, still writing our story

Never invite anyone else in, keeping everyone else
out
Remember that it is a sacred union and we must be
devout!

The marriage bed must not be taken lightly,
For the Almighty God, will not judge slightly, but
rightly

Yes, the marriage bed is a secret sacred place,
The holy acts of love done there, cannot be disgraced

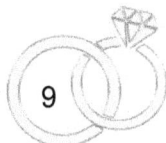

Romance

Let's keep the romance alive
between me and you
Let's work to help it thrive
by doing what we need to do

Let's keep the romance burning
fanning the flames day by day, month by month
Let's keep our hearts earnestly yearning
so it doesn't get filled with junk

Let's keep the romance going
even through bitter times and pain
For those are the times God will be showing
that through his name we can reign

Let's keep the romance kindled
through disappointments that life brings
So that the sparks will not dwindle
through the tests and trials of various things

Let's keep the romance spicy
By being attentive and showing we care
Let's not become complacent and lazy
But by work and effort, show that we are really there

Let's give our romance the ultimate chance
Bit by bit, situation by situation
By loving life and taking a rewarding dance
Step by step, in this adventurous marital formation

Fidelity

Fidelity means being faithful in the sacred union called, marriage

Fidelity means being loyal and taking a good strong dose of courage

Fidelity means being true to your spouse in your heart & down to your soul

Fidelity means being honest to ensure the trust bond is not stole

Fidelity means sharing yourself exclusively only with your mate

Fidelity means exclusivity and not even entertaining an outside date

Fidelity means no flirting around and no, not a kiss

Fidelity means your lips are sealed and the divorce court you will miss

Fidelity means commitment to your spouse, to your spouse alone

Fidelity means practicing self constraint ensuring you'll still have a home.

Fidelity means two people and there's no room for three,

Fidelity means a promise to be true, I with you and you with me

Fidelity means peace between the woman and the man

Fidelity means no shame because they've both taken a stand

Fidelity means sacredness upon the marital bed

Fidelity means a holy bond that is based on what God has said

Vows

Vows are promises made before God and man
They are words spoken into the atmosphere
assuming to stand

Vows are oaths uttered from the heart and from the
lips
They are capsules of creative force, that we can't let
slip

Vows are pledges spoken to one another
They are declarations of love that should make one
shudder

Vows are commitments to daily lay down our life
Such commitments can only be realized through the
Lord Jesus Christ.

Vows are the swearing to your own hurt, to protect
your beloved
They are heartfelt convictions that are rendered to a
spouse thereof

Vows are covenant agreements shared between two
They are sworn statements to relinquish whatever is
due

Vows are bonds created when heart to heart words
are spoken

They are words that catch the ears of God so we can't
be joking
Vows are words of honor in which, we say what we
mean and mean what we say
They are words of truth and integrity spoken to each
other, just like when we pray

Being a Wife

Being a wife is quite a job,
I can't fulfill it by being a snob
I must humble myself day by day,
in order to do this the bible way

I committed to be a loving wife,
I know I must make some sacrifice
Saying yes, when I don't want to,
Knowing God will see me through

I clean the kitchen and I wash the clothes,
The other things I do, only heaven knows
I feed the babies and put them to sleep,
My prayer to God is my mind he'll keep

I walk with my husband side by side,
because I made the promise to be his bride
Our life together it's not perfect,
we work together to make it worth it

Sometimes in life we don't agree
But that doesn't mean that we can't be,
Loving and kind for the most part,
I thank God He knows our hearts

Being a Husband

Being a husband is a Godly position,
I will even say that it is a mission

It's more than just being a man,
It's being committed and taking a stand

Taking care of my wife means responsibility,
Making sure... really sure that she has stability

It's being attentive and filled with romance,
It's being united as we go through life's dance

Being a husband means being kind and faithful,
It's not being bitter, not being hateful

It's listening to God, so I can fulfill my role,
It's listening to her, so I can protect her soul

It's washing the dishes or the clothes,
Doing what I can to lighten her load

It's being there and showing appreciation,
It's being there in a humble demonstration

Being a husband means being there to minimize
frustration,
It's being there to bring love and confirmation

1986

1986, you broke my heart,
You literally tried to tear my life apart
You almost took my marriage, you made me cry
You took my momma, I felt I wanted to die

I prayed and prayed, but heaven seemed like brass,
I was broken and disgusted, I had no cash
The babe in the womb would come that year,
It was the greatest thing that brought me cheer

Grief and sorrow tried to take my life,
I'm so glad for Yeshua, Jesus Christ
For he would not let either of them win,
he's my victory over grief and sin

1986, though you dealt me some crushing blows,
Yes, you brought me down really low
Today, I stand. I stand in Jesus Christ,
Restored and Blessed in my God's sight

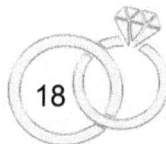

Jealousy

Jealousy… Jealousy, you're a cruel old witch,
I need to whip and defeat you with a strong willow
switch
With a willow switch, I'll whip you so low
Yes, I will render to you a cruel crushing blow

You lied to me…you lied to me and made me feel
bad,
You told me I was ugly and nearly drove me mad
You have twisted the way that I see myself,
You've exhausted me mentally, until I had nothing left

You've made me fear the real woman that I am,
While you've exalted and lifted every Pam and
Madame!

You tempt me to rage about what I ain't
I'm so tired of you sometimes I feel faint

You work overtime to convince me of what I am not,
I have to remember that I've been bought

With the willow switch of my God's word,
I will break you in sunder with what I have heard

I have heard in his word that you are a weapon
A weapon that shall not prosper
Therefore, what you've tried to do to me is spiritually
improper

Knowing this, I put you on notice and I declare to you
your prognosis
I am dead to you and you to me,
Now, I can plainly see

That I have the power to kick you out of my life,
Through the word, the blood, and authority of Yeshua,
Jesus Christ!

Beware of the Competitive Goddess

The competitive goddess seeks to take your man,
Yes, she will break up your family if she can
She's as loud…loud as all get out,
She comes to deceive and reduce you to doubt
She wants to intimidate the wife of a man,
Always wanting to prove that she is better than
Inwardly, she is very mean,
And Honey, you know she's got to be seen
She's pushy and demands to be heard,
I say to you, this is quite absurd
Her clothes…her clothes are worn so tight,
Now girl, you know that just ain't right
She flatters with her words and bats her eyes,
She walks with a switch, down the aisle she strides
Lust and adultery are in her heart,
She disguises her motives, thinking you're not smart
Beware of her…Beware of her and take care of your soul,
All she is after, is a little fun and gold

Here Comes Slick

Now Slick…he's a bible toter,
If you're not careful, he might be a groper

He can quote more scripture than you can believe,
deep in his heart, he seeks to deceive

He'll get you off track, off of the word,
Talking about he loves you, which is just absurd

He knows nothing about (Yeshua) Jesus Christ,
he'll play the role and you will pay the price

So wise up girl and don't be a fool,
Girl, just know today, that you've been schooled

If he's all that and a bag of chips,
Why are those women still on his hip?

He tells you he has more to offer than your husband,
Girl, take a look, he's standing on quicksand

Now, God has already blessed you with a spouse,
Will you choose to run after a mouse?

A mouse that squeaks with deceit, intending to trick
you out of your soul,
He will play you like a pimp, drain you of all your gold

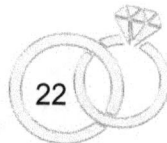

Now you're left with nothing,
Not one blessed thing

Not a marriage, not a home,
And when you look for old Slick,
          Honey, he's gone to another home!

Pain

Pain, Pain, you hurt...so bad,
You strain my life and make me sad
You're as sharp as a knife down in my soul,
You really hate when I feel whole

You bring hurt and hurt through wrong perception,
Try to mix me up, with your spirit of deception
You tear me down, down with lying distortion,
You really want this marriage to have an abortion

You try to blind our eyes so we can't see,
See the good in him and in me
You work over time to lie, lie, lie
Causing anguish in our souls that we should cry

Pain, Pain, you want to reign,
I tell you today, that you're insane
Let me say it well and make it plain,
My God has given me the name, Elaine

So my name is Elaine, my husband's name is Willie,
Though we've had some cold nights, some that were
chilly
I need you to know this thing sincerely and really
That God is our mainstay and he'll keep us from being
silly.

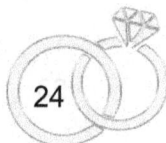

Be Patient

Be Patient, Be Patient, you husband and wife,
Be careful not to get into stewing strife

Be Patient, Be Patient, love all the way,
For if you're not patient, old satan will sway

Be Patient and know that marriage is not instant,
It has to go through fire to remain in existence

Be Patient and don't let your tempers reign,
Remember, in marriage you will have some pain

Be Patient, Be Patient, don't pack your bags,
No, not a stitch, not even a rag

Be patient, Be Patient, go sit in a room
One heated argument doesn't mean the marriage is
doomed!

Be patient, Be Patient, watch what you say,
If you want your marriage to last, beyond today

Be Patient, Be patient for no one is without flaw
Careful to remember that love is your law

Be patient, My Dear, don't get in a huff
Don't start screaming, about getting a divorce

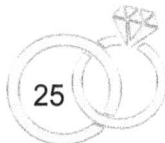

Be patient and know that patience is a virtue
Be patient and know that God has chosen you

Be patient and remember that haste makes waste
Be patient, Be patient with humbleness you can win
this race

Build Me Up

Build me up, Build me up my earthly and chosen king,
For the word of God says, that I'm your good thing

Build me up, for you will obtain favor from the Lord,
Build me up, I promise we won't be bored

Build me up, Build me up before you build another,
Remember that, I come first and not any other

Build me up, I promise to be your queen,
Build me up, I promise not to be mean, I'm here to
uplift and help fulfill your dreams

Build me up, Build me up my dearest reverent wife,
Please, don't let your words feel like a knife
Don't strip away my manhood, don't cut me down like
a dog,
Then walk away leaving, my head in a fog

Build me up, Build me up and you will see,
I'll do more than leap over tall buildings just for thee,
Build me up, I will be that man
Simply because, by your words, I can stand

Build me up, Build me up, I will be the man you want
and need,
Build me up, Build me up and I can definitely
succeed!

Cancer

Cancer, Cancer came one day,
You know, it really wanted to stay
We and God said, "No...No...No!"
Cancer, Cancer you got to go!

We prayed and prayed for direction,
Refused to let cancer prolong its session
One day, one day the answer came,
We knew we had direction and victory, in Jesus Name

God's wisdom was to go to the surgeon,
by this time the case was urgent
My husband submitted to God on the throne and the
surgeon on earth,
To God, his creator, who knew his worth!

Afterwards, the prognosis was good, he needed to
rest,
The surgeon had worked and did his best
Now God would once more show that he was reallier,
By manifesting that he was still a healer

Cancer, Cancer we bid you farewell,
Frankly, you can return to the place called, hell
Henceforth, please stay from whence you came,
For we are standing on Jesus' stripes and his blood
stains

2014

2014 was a year of glory
Behold, be still, let me tell my story
It started, It started with answers to prayer
Heaven poured out blessings, God deemed fair

One son stepped out in faith
To get his dream house
We got the news and we all did shout
But wait a minute! For God wasn't through
He had more blessings for us too

So we stepped out, dream house in mind
List already made, believing God would be kind
We looked and looked at just three
But knew the one, that was meant to be

It matched the list that was made
So I was confident and not afraid
We signed the contract and made the deal
God showed his glory, showed he was real

Another son stepped out, to get his dream truck
And listen, what happened was not merely luck
They negotiated, talked, and made a deal
Needless to say, the son was really thrilled

God answers prayer, Oh, can't you see?
This story, this story is not just about me
It's about the Almighty, that he will answer you
If you dare to invite him and acknowledge him in all
you do

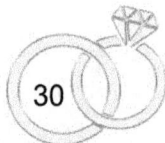

Taking a Stand

This precious union between a woman and a man,
Requires both of them to take, a firm stand

Stand up, Stand up for each other,
Stand up, Stand up against the pressures of another

Say what needs to be said and do what needs to be done,
For, it's both of your responsibility to make sure the victory is won

You're now bone of bone and flesh of flesh,
It's your job to make sure, that no one starts any mess

You must forsake all others and put one another first,
This is the key component, to ensure you don't fall under a curse

You're for him and he's for you,
Now work together to do your best due

Be careful not to let the opinions of others, create a breach,
Remember that togetherness, is the lesson that God does teach

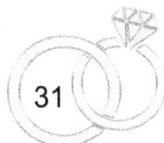

Be strong and stand up for your relationship,
Stand up and let it be known that this is your partnership

If you don't stand up, no one else will,
When you stand up, God will be a manifested shield

Guard your relationship and treat it with care,
By doing so, perhaps your spouse will always be there

Close every door, curve every C and dot every I,
This can help safeguard your marriage and prove the devil is a lie

Don't allow someone to speak negatively about your spouse,
Stand up, don't be afraid, for it's no time to be a mouse

When someone comes to your home and acts disrespectful,
Stand up, show them the door, for it's no time to be regretful
Stand up and don't be a coward when the rubber meets the road,
This is a test of your strength and loyalty, so sometimes you have to be bold

Stand up for the gift, you've been given,
For God wants to shine in marriage and give you a life
worth living

Mother-In-Laws

Mother-In-Laws, Mother-In-Laws
Do you know your place?
Position yourself to go to the throne of grace,
So your son and daughter can win this race
Stop so much talking, about what you wouldn't do,
Remember this is their relationship and it ain't about
you
Granted you are able to give advice,
But be careful to do it, do it very nice

You didn't lose a son, but gained a daughter,
So please treat her the way you outta'
You didn't lose a daughter, but gained a son,
So open your eyes and see you have won

You have two now, instead of one,
So listen to me, cause I'm not done.
They will care for you and love you too,
So be kind and respectful, in all you do.

So if you let their relationship be,
Then you will be able to plainly see
That heaven indeed, has smiled upon you,
And given you a blessing, that is uniquely new

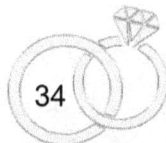

In Laws, Out Laws?

You didn't like me from the start,
Your looks and words broke my heart
You didn't even give me a chance,
To show that I was more than a temporary
circumstance

You smiled, but your heart was far away,
In your thoughts, I knew you wanted me to go astray
But I stood, I stood on my God's word,
I stood and stood on what I had heard

You never thought I was good enough,
You treated me ill and sometimes rough
You hinted about exes of the past,
You made me feel our marriage couldn't last

With your words you brought me to nought,
But in my secret place, the Lord I sought
I sought him with fasting and with prayer,
through it all, I refused to swear

Then one day God turned things around,
I realized that I was no longer bound
Love and acceptance, it prevailed,
God showed me that his word never fails

Now In-Laws are indeed in-laws,
and Out-law behavior is exed out
For this, I can truly shout!

I have In-Laws that love me and I love them the same,
Today, I'm standing in God's glory, in Jesus (Yeshua)'s Name

Raising

I'm not raising him,
He's not raising me
The answer is embracing,
Both now and in eternity

So, no more of this, "You will do and I told you…"
Like a drill sergeant in command,
But instead, "Honey, will you and thank you..."
From a humble God-fearing man

No more as a wife will I say, "You better!"
Or give you a demanding evil eye
When you hurt my feelings,
I will sit, pray, and sigh

I won't tell you what time to go to bed,
you won't tell me what time to get up
Realizing we have both been raised,
now we kneel at God's throne to sup

Here is the conclusion
To this warped illusion
I'm not raising him
He's not raising me
Together we walk, learn, and discern
That the Father, He is the key

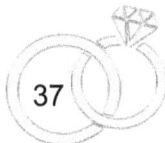

Forgiveness

Forgiveness is an act, an act of your will,
an act that you don't immediately feel

Forgiveness is releasing the anguish and pain,
doing it by Faith in Jesus (Yeshua) Name

Forgiveness is giving up the right to be right,
the guilt of being wrong
It is the act of running swiftly to God's merciful throne

Admitting it all before Jesus Christ
Knowing confidently that he has paid the price
The price over bitterness, anger, and strife,
The price that was indeed divinely suffice

Only through God's son, Jesus Christ,
we don't have to lose our marital life

Learn to forgive and do it quick,
because you know that the enemy is slick

For he will cheat you out of your marriage,
leaving you with a disadvantage

Remember that forgiveness is an act of your will,
without it your relationship will become ill

Without forgiveness, the enemy will undoubtedly steal,
but with it, God is able to seal and heal

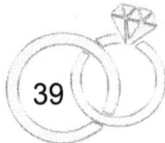

Strife

Strife, Strife your contentions are sharp as a knife,
How have you come to set a man against his wife?

The wife of his youth and his old age,
You're quite intrusive with your terrible rage

Strife, Strife you come to steal, kill, and destroy,
a lesson you will learn, you treacherous and hateful
boy

Strife, Strife you stir up mess and ugly pride,
you must remember, we have the Lord on our side

You're messy, triflin', and you just don't care,
You don't care how many years that we've been there

Strife, Strife you come to divide and conquer,
all because you are a horrible monster

I tell you today, that you will not win,
because we have the cure for this horrific sin

It's all in the blood, the blood of Jesus Christ,
As you well know, He was the ultimate sacrifice

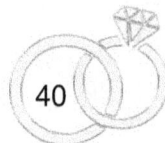

Peace

Peace is tranquility
Giving you the ability
To live without hostility
Weathering all adversity

Peace is the absence of chaos
It helps to avoid heated face-offs'
With Peace you won't need milky Maalox
Because you decided to let peace be boss

If you seek peace and seek it well
You can avoid confusion and living in hell (chaos)

Seek peace, seek it in all you do
It is the virtue that will see you through
Shut up, be quiet, and get the clue
Understand, the love that your spouse has for you

Peace is the ability to reach your goals
The substance that can really make you whole
Tranquility and calmness will fill your soul
It is a gift from God, so I'm told

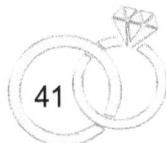

Never a Crossword?

Never a crossword, you say...
I find it hard to believe
Are you telling the truth?
Or, do you seek to deceive?

Twenty or more years together and never a fuss?
No mixing of words, either or lifting your voice?
I can believe that perhaps you didn't cuss,
but never a crossword, I wonder by choice or by
force?

Two people from two pathways of life
I know communication won't always be right
Good intentions, but remarks don't come out correct
I'm sorry, I'm sorry that my words upset

You want to go, I want to stay home
I may not say it, but could you please just go on
You want me to give up, yield to your will
but I hear a voice say, "Just be still"

What's not said in words, are said in deeds
I may sit in silence then give you the eye
Can you pay attention and learn to read?
Because I'm as cross as cross can be,
though I sit in silence, wondering why with a sigh

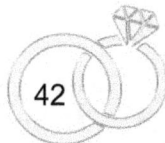

So when you say to me, we've never had a crossword
I would have to say, I have never heard
Heard of two people living in marriage together
Having not a cross action, attitude, or word, no, not
never!

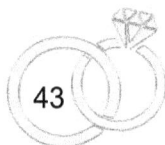

Intimacy

Look into me, into me and you will see
the beauty that is bottled inside
My potential, possibilities that cannot be denied

Look into me, into me and you will see
the scars that have warped myself imagery
and the scars that have affected my identity

Look into me, into me and you will see
a scared little girl with numerous fears
Who needs someone to embrace her and wipes away
her tears

Look into me, into me and you will see
a beautiful treasure so full of worth
That needs someone to value and to help unearth

Look into me, into me and you will see
A little boy so marred with rejection
Because he didn't have a dad to give the right
reflection

Look into me, into me and you will see
Insecurities, but bravery and courage
Hoping that you are the right one to help me heal and
flourish.

Look into me, into me and you will see
If you talk to me and not at me
I will open up and show you, who I can really be

Look into me, into me and you will see
If you spend time with me, I will rise out of obscurity
and reach my full potentiality.

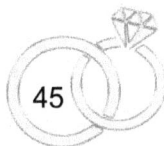

You Have to Get Out of that Bed!

When physical intimacy is over and done,
how will you both relate?
Will you pack your bags and run, run, run,
or, still be a respectful and loving mate?

You see it's easy to be physical,
it doesn't take much of a heart at all
This act of passion is simply not unusual,
when it's over, will you still answer the commitment
call?

We give ourselves to one another,
In such a close and intimate way
In that moment, anger and resentment we smother,
when it's over, will you have the guts to stay?

Will we talk to each other in tender love,
or, speak sharply, hatefully, and mean?
Will we allow God's conviction, thereof,
to be right there on the scene?

We must learn to speak love language,
Beyond the physical and the bed
So that our relationship won't languish,
Nor, our hearts grow cold and dead

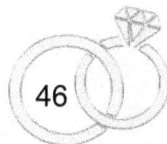

Marriages Made in Heaven

Marriages may indeed be made in Heaven
However, they must be worked out on Earth
Sometimes you'll have to inhale, then count to seven
To remember that you have the power of the new
birth

The meshing of two lives together, is quite a daunting
task
Therefore, you must stay on the potter's wheel
If indeed, you want the marital relationship to last
You'll be able to see God's plan and will fulfilled

In marriage, there will definitely be problems
Please, don't pray for them not to come
Instead, pray for heavenly wisdom to solve them,
and realize where the problems originate from.

Yes, God has ordained marriage to help with
loneliness
Thus, in order for it to work, it has to have
humbleness
The forsaking and renouncing of pride and me, me,
me
Yielding to a spirit that is contrite and broken that is
willing to seek after thee

We don't have to worry, for Heaven will do its part
we must be willing to relinquish an unrepentant heart

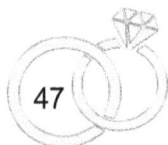

God's spirit is always present and always on the scene
If we acknowledge and invite him, he will surely intervene.

God will work with us, as we work together,
To make our marriage sound and whole
He will hear and answer us, whenever,
problems try to invade and destroy our marital soul

Marriages made in heaven, must operate like this
Solicit God's help, operate in humbleness, forgiveness, and less pridefulness
Work together, putting in the time, the effort, and the tears
The end result will perhaps be, a relationship that will last for years

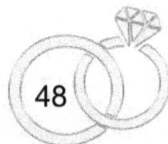

Money, Money

Money, money in the marital relationship,
poorly managed, can lead to a deep rip

God knows that we all need money,
be careful not to let it spoil you, Honey!

Though money is the median of exchange,
Be careful, it can cause your life to be totally
rearranged

From happily married to drastically divorced,
you allowed money to get you off course

Whether too little, well...it can sink you,
or, too much, well... it can ruin you

Money should never be your marital measuring stick,
Having it or not having it, please, don't let it make you
sick

If you need money, just follow the word,
Tithe and give offerings is what I've heard

Do the word and the word will see you through,
poverty and lack, won't know what to do

Don't spend your time fussing about money,
Just roll up your sleeves and go to work, Honey

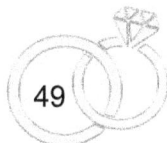

Don't be a statistic, fighting about finance,
Just be diligent, so you can keep your romance

Manage what you have and don't junk it off,
Be a wise steward and compare every cost

Don't try to live beyond your means,
There's nothing wrong, with eating cornbread and
beans

As you be faithful and follow God's principles,
He will lift you financially, beyond what is naturally
sensible

Money, money, don't you let it rule,
Remember God's wisdom is your success tool

Money, money, don't let it break up your home,
Don't make it an idol or you just might be alone

Just Because

Just because I don't see what you see
Doesn't mean, I don't love you

Just because I don't feel what you feel
Doesn't mean, I don't love you

Just because I don't agree with you
Doesn't mean, I don't love you.

Just because I don't hear what you hear
Doesn't mean, I don't love you.

Just because I don't perceive what you perceive
Doesn't mean, I don't love you.

Just because I don't eat what you eat
Doesn't mean, I don't love you.

Just because I don't express love the way you do
Doesn't mean, I don't love you.

Just because I don't think the way you do
Doesn't mean, I don't love you.

Just because I don't have the same convictions you
do
Doesn't mean, I don't love you.

Just because...Just because...Just because…
All the becauses…
Doesn't mean, I don't love you.

A Bed of Roses?

Marriage is not a bed of roses,
I don't know who could've told ya'

I'm here to help you discern truth from fiction,
in this thing called marriage, you're going to have
friction

You will have some seasons of unwarranted trouble,
and other seasons you will have guaranteed double

You have to take the good with the bad,
And yeah, sometimes it might even make you mad

You have to take the bitter with the sweet,
You have to steady yourself and do what's meet

Some days you will laugh and some days you will cry,
There will be dark days, which you feel like you will
die

Marriage can be exciting and so filled with joy,
It can also be filled with disappointments and things
that annoy

In marriage, you will face challenges, things you must
overcome
So gird up the lions of your mind, cause' you're not
dumb.

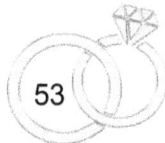

Some days you'll want to shout and tell the whole world
Some days you'll be filled with anguish because what life has hurled

Marriage is a journey the two of you take together
But that doesn't mean, you won't have some bad weather

Remember that marriage, is not a bed of roses and please, remember the thorns
Don't forget that the enemy will surely show up, with his huge ugly horns

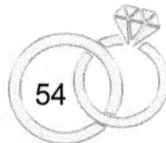

Dwell Together in Knowledge

When we dwell together in knowledge, we are spending ample time together to get to know one another. We are making it our business to put our relationship first before any other.

When we dwell together in knowledge, we are walking in commitment to meet one another's needs. We are deliberately planning and searching for ways to help our relationship succeed.

When we dwell together in knowledge, we learn not to take each other for granted. We believe in the mission of marriage and strive to bloom where we have been planted.

When we dwell in knowledge, there are no big I's and little U's. We realize that our success depends on the concept, not of "you do" but of "we do."

Dwelling in knowledge means we're willing to sit down and put on our listening ears. Knowing that the time we spend hashing things out can yield us many years.

Dwelling in knowledge means we've learned what each of us like and what annoys. It also means we both have gained a good understanding of the things we do enjoy.

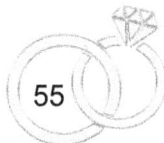

Dwelling in knowledge means we are careful of what we say and do. We embrace and accept the fact that I am me and you, are you.

Dwelling in knowledge means living, abiding, staying together, and even more. Realizing that marriage means work, putting forth effort, and yes, sometimes it is even a chore

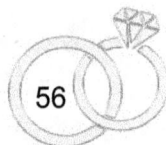

Pleased to Dwell?

If he's knocking you around, is he pleased to dwell?
If you're sitting in the emergency room, with your face
and lip swelled?

If he's cussing you out and calling you every name
under the sun...
If he's standing over you and in his hand is a gun, is
he pleased to dwell?

If he's got you hemmed in a corner, you can't breathe
and he's daring you, daring you to even attempt to
sneeze, is he pleased to dwell?

If he's being unfaithful and to you, brought a disease
Just tell me, tell me is this person pleased, is he
pleased to dwell?

If she's slapping you in your face, and berating you
like a mouse
Tell me if she's pleased for you to be in that house?
Is she pleased to dwell?

If she's provoking you to hit her, so she can call the
police
Just know she wants you locked up and never to be
released, is she pleased to dwell?

If she's sleeping around with different people in the town
Realize, Realize that this girl ain't sound, is she pleased to dwell?

If the unbeliever be pleased to dwell,
the believer shall not put them away
This shouldn't mean the believer has to live in hell (chaos)
For rightly dividing the word, will help determine if the unbeliever should go or stay

Pleased to dwell? Pleased to dwell?
I Corinthians the 7th chapter
Please consult it on this matter

Servant to Servant

As we walk this road together,
We walk it side by side

Learning each day to humble ourselves,
Allowing God's grace and love to abide

Servant to servant is the attitude and mindset,
For which we must be committed and be tied

We have to learn to put away all foolishness,
and every stupid pride

I must serve you and you should me, as your earthly
bride
If we do these things, our relationship's success will
not be denied

Sometimes we may jump in the car and take a brief
joyride
Sometimes we might sit and enjoy chicken that has
been fried

Love each other, Love each other is what the Lord
has replied
We know from the scriptures, that He won't always
chide

As we live as a servant or helper in the place where
we reside,

It will help to lessen the opportunities for the enemy to divide

Serve each other, Serve each other and to one another confide
Serve each other, Serve each other by doing this, the Lord will be glorified